A Collector's Guide
HEISEY ORCHID ETCH

Donald R. Oksa

MW00558971

Schiffer Publishing Ltd

4880 Lower Valley Road, Atglen, PA 19310 USA

Dedication

This book of Heisey Orchid Etch is very respectfully dedicated to the memory of Mavis N. Oksa. Without her dedication to collecting Heisey there would not have been a collection at all.

Published by Schiffer Publishing Ltd.
4880 Lower Valley Road
Atglen, PA 19310
Phone: (610) 593-1777; Fax: (610) 593-2002
E-mail: Info@schifferbooks.com

For the largest selection of fine reference books on this and related subjects, please visit our web site at
www.schifferbooks.com
We are always looking for people to write books on new and related subjects. If you have an idea for a book please contact us at the above address.

This book may be purchased from the publisher.
Include $3.95 for shipping.
Please try your bookstore first.
You may write for a free catalog.

In Europe, Schiffer books are distributed by
Bushwood Books
6 Marksbury Ave.
Kew Gardens
Surrey TW9 4JF England
Phone: 44 (0) 20 8392-8585; Fax: 44 (0) 20 8392-9876
E-mail: info@bushwoodbooks.co.uk
Website: www.bushwoodbooks.co.uk
Free postage in the U.K., Europe; air mail at cost.

Covers and book designed by: Bruce Waters
Type set in City and Arrus

ISBN: 0-7643-2514-0
Printed in China

Acknowledgments

Computer Assistance: Donald L. Oksa

Photography: Terry R. Oksa & Jerry R. Oksa

Moral Support: Judy D. Oksa Thome

Contents

Introduction

It hardly seems possible that almost twenty-five years have passed since my wife and I were first introduced to the Heisey line of glassware and, in particular, the Orchid Etch part of the line.

My wife loved flowering plants and grew many varieties, among which her special favorites were orchids. When, in 1982, our son Jerry brought home a few pieces of Heisey Orchid Etch he had found in Powell, Wyoming. they almost immediately became her very favorite thing to go on about. We had become collectors.

The Orchid Etch pattern was first introduced by Heisey in 1940 and within a few years had become one of their leading lines. It was well received by the public and expanded to include over 200 items. Orchid Etch was applied to a wide range of forms from Heisey's glass lines, including Graceful, Tyrolean, Princess, Queen Ann, Waverly, Fern, Lariat, and more. In fact, after the company went out of business in 1957, the Imperial Glass Company, who took over the operation, intermittently filled orders for Orchid Etch into 1961 and 1962.

We do not have the entire line at our disposal. When possible we have substituted drawings from the company catalogs and brochures. In a few cases, we show the same pattern, but with no etch or maybe a different etch. In still other cases, we have resorted to using a crude sketch of the item.

Our goal has been to represent all of the pieces of the Orchid Etch line of which we are aware, and we have come close to doing just that.

As you will note there are measurements accompanying most of the images. These measurements are not "cast in stone," but are reasonably close and made with simple scales.

Occasionally in the descriptions we find the term "footed." It is vague as to what type. In order to avoid this ambiguity we have used the three terms to describe what type: pedestal-footed, fan-footed, and dolphin-footed. These are illustrated in the following three pictures.

Pedestal-footed

ORDINARY ABBREVIATIONS

d = diameter
dt = diameter of top
db = diameter of bottom
dcc = diameter of the clear center of a plate or bowl
h = height
w = width
l = length
sq = Square
mxd = maximum diameter
(no picture) = not available at this time
Ind = Individual
S&C = sugar and creamer

HEISEY NAME ABREVIATIONS

AC = Aqua Caliente
CV = Covington
DO = Donna
DQ = Duguenne
FE = Fern
GR = Graceful
LA = Lariat
NA = National
OX = Oxford
PR = Princess
QA = Queen Ann
TY = Tyrolean
VL = Velvedure
WV = Waverly
YO = Yeoman

Dolphin-footed

Fan-footed

Glasses

5022 Graceful Goblet, 10 oz., tall stem. 8-1/2" h, 2-7/8"
dt, 3-1/16" db. $50.00

5025 Tyrolean Goblet, 10 oz., tall stem. 8-1/2" h, 2-7/8"
dt, 3-1/16" db. $50.00

Comparison Graceful and Tyrolean Goblets,
10 oz., tall stems.

5022 Graceful Goblet, 10 oz., short stem. 6" h, 2-7/8"
dt, 3-1/16" db. $50.00

5089 Princess Goblet, 10 oz., short stem. 5-1/2" h,
3-5/8" dt, 3" db, only 1 knurl. $120.00

5025 Tyrolean Goblet, 10 oz., short stem. 6-3/16" h,
3-7/16" dt, 3-1/16" db. $50.00

Comparison of 10 oz., short stem goblets. Graceful, Tyrolean, and Princess.

5022 Graceful Saucer Champagne, 6 oz. 6-3/16" h,
4-1/8" dt, 3-1/16" db. $45.00

5026 Tyrolean Saucer Champagne, 6 oz. 6-3/16" h,
4-1/8" dt, 3-1/16" db. $45.00

5089 Princess Saucer Champagne 5-1/2 oz. *Not illustrated.* $120.00

Comparison of Graceful and Tyrolean Saucer Champagnes, 6 oz., Graceful & Tyrolean.

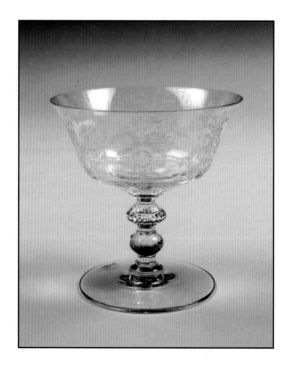

5022 Graceful Sherbet, 6 oz.
4" h, 4" dt, 3" db. $55.00

5025 Tyrolean Sherbet, 6 oz. 4" h, 4" dt, 3" db. $55.00

Comparison of 6 oz. Graceful and Tyrolean Sherbets.

5022 Graceful Claret, 4-1/2 oz. (converted to a bell).
5-1/4" h as is, 2-1/4" dt. $90.00

5025 Tyrolean Claret, 4-1/2 oz. 6-3/8" h, 2-5/8" dt,
3-1/2" db. $90.00

14

5089 Princess Claret, 4 oz. *Not illustrated.* $130.00

Comparison of Graceful and Tyrolean Claret shapes.

5022 Graceful Cocktail, 4 oz. 5-1/2" h, 3-1/4" dt,
2-1/2" db. $45.00

5025 Tyrolean Cocktail, 4 oz. 5-1/2" h, 3-1/4" dt, 2-1/2" db. $45.00

4002 Aqua Caliente Cocktail, 4 oz. 4-1/2" h, 2-3/16" dt, 2-1/8" db. $100.00

5089 Princess Cocktail, 3-1/2 oz. *Not illustrated.* $120.00

Comparison Graceful, Tyrolean, and Aqua Caliente Cocktails.

5022 Graceful Oyster Cocktail 4 oz. 3-3/4" h, 2-11/16" dt, 1-7/16" db. $50.00

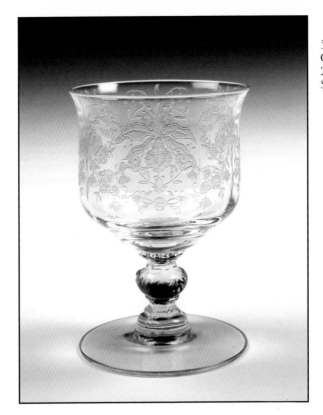

5025 Tyrolean Oyster Cocktail, 4 oz. 3-3/4" h, 2-11/16" dt, 1-7/16" db. $50.00

5089 Princess Oyster Cocktail, 2-1/2 oz. *Not illustrated.* $110.00

Comparison Graceful and Tyrolean Oyster Cocktails, 4 oz.

5022 Graceful Wine, 3 oz. 5-3/8" h,
1-7/8" dt, 2" db. $80.00

5025 Tyrolean Wine, 3 oz. 5-1/4" h, 2-1/4"
dt, 2-1/16" db. $80.00

5089 Princess Wine, 2-1/2 oz. *Not illustrated.* $95.00

Comparison of Graceful and Tyrolean Wines, 3 oz.

5022 Graceful Sherry, 2 oz. 5-3/8" h, 2-1/4"
dt, 2-1/8" db. $115.00

5025 Tyrolean Sherry, 2 oz. 5-3/8" h, 2-1/4"
dt, 2-1/8" db. $85.00

3311 Velvadure Sherry, 2-1/2 oz. 5-1/2" h,
2-1/4" dt, 2-1/16" db. $175.00

4090 Coventry Sherry, 2 oz. 5-3/16" h, 2-3/4" dt. $80.00

5022 Graceful Cordial, 1 oz. 5-1/4" h,
2" dt, 1-15/16" db. $100.00

4090 Coventry Cordial, 1 oz. *Not illustrated.* $200.00

5025 Tyrolean Cordial, 1 oz. 5-1/4" h,
2" dt, 1-15/16" db. $100.00

5089 Princess Cordial, 1 oz. . 4-1/2" h, 1-1/2"
dt, 1-7/8". $200.00

5024 Oxford Cordial, 1 oz. 350 made in 1978. 3-1/2" h, 1-5/8" dt, 2" db. $150.00

Comparison of Graceful, Tyrolean, Oxford, and Princess Cordials.

5022 Graceful Juice 5 oz. 5-7/16" h, 2-1/4"
dt, 2-1/4" db. $65.00

5025 Tyrolean Juice, 5 oz. 5-7/16" h, 2-3/8"
dt, 3-1/16" db. $65.00

5089 Princess Juice, 5 oz. *Not illustrated.* $140.00

Comparison Juice Graceful and Tyrolean Juices, 5 oz.

5022 Graceful Juice, 12 oz. 6-1/2" h, 2-3/4" dt, 3-1/4" db. $75.00

5025 Tyrolean Juice, 12 oz. 6-3/4" h, 3-15/16"
dt, 3-1/16" db. $75.00

5089 Princess Juice, 12 oz. 6-3/8" h, 3-1/4"
dt, 2-7/8" db. $80.00

Comparison Graceful, Tyrolean, and Princess Juices 12 oz.

5022 Graceful Dinner Bell, converted
from a 4-1/2 oz. claret. $90.00

5025 Tyrolean Dinner Bell, converted from
a 4-1/2 oz. claret. $90.00

5025 Tyrolean Dinner Bell from a 10 oz.,
tall goblet. $90.00

5025 Tyrolean Dinner Bell from a
3 oz. wine. $90.00

Comparison Graceful and Tyrolean Dinner Bells.

2052 Bar Glass, 2 oz. 2-3/8" h, 1-1-15/16" dt, 1-3/8" db. $95.00

Left: 2351 Newton Soda Glass, 6 oz. 4" h, 2-1/4" dt, 1-7/8" db, 0.2125 taper. $75.00
Right: 2401 Oakwood Soda Glass, Sahara, 6 oz. 4" h, 2-1/4" dt, 1-5/8" db, 0-5/16" taper. $75.00

Left: 2351 Newton Soda Glass, 7 oz. 4" h, 2-1/4" dt, 1-7/8" db. $75.00
Right: 2401 Oakwood Soda Glass, 7 oz. 4-1/8" h, 2-1/2" dt, 1-7/8" db, 0-5/16" taper. $75.00

Left: 2351 Newton Soda Glass, 12 oz. 5-1/8" h, 2-3/4" dt, 2-1/4" db, 0-1/4" taper. $75.00
Right: 2401 Oakwood Soda Glass, TallyHo, 12 oz. 5-1/8" h, 2-3/4" dt, 2.00" db, 0-3/8" taper. $75.00

34

Comparison 2351 Newton Soda Glasses, 7 oz., 12 oz., 6 oz.

Comparison of 2401 Oakwood Soda Glasses, 7oz,12 oz., 6 oz.

4052 National Soda Glass, 10 oz. 5-1/8" h,
2-3/4" dt, 2-1/4" db. $50.00

3484 Donna Soda Glass, 12 oz. 5" h, 3-3/8"
dt, 1-1/2" d at 5/8" h, 2-3/4" db. $50.00

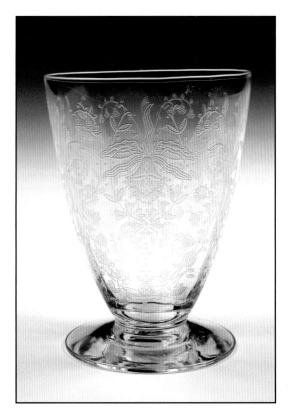

3389 Duquesne Soda Glass, 10 oz. 5-1/4" h, 3-3/8" dt, 1-1/2"d at 5/8" h, 2-3/4" db. $50.00

Comparison of Donna, Duquesne, and National Soda

Plates

Sandwich Plate with 'T' handle

1435 Ash Tray. 3"
square. $30.00

1519 Waverly Saucer. 5-7/8" d. Note the 1-3/4" diameter clear center. $55.00

1509 Queen Ann Saucer. 6-1/4" d. Note the 1-3/8""
diameter clear center. $35.00

ComparisonQueen Ann and Waverly Saucers.

1509 Queen Ann Cup and Saucer. Saucer: 6-1/4"
d; Cup: 2.19 d, 3.19" dt. Wavy top. $55.00

1519 Waverly Cup and Saucer. Saucer: 5-7/8" d; Cup: 2.88 d,
3-3/4 dt; vert dots. $55.00

Comparison Waverly and Queen Ann Cups and Saucers.

1519 Waverly 7 inch Salad Plate.
7-1/4" d, 4-3/8" dcc. $35.00

1519 Waverly 8 inch Salad
Plate. 8-1/4" d, 3 dcc, $20.00

1495 Fern Mayonnaise Plate, 8 d. 7-5/8" w x 9" l, one handled. $45.00

1519 Waverly 7 inch Mayonnaise Plate.
7-1/4" d, 2-7/8" d, raised ring. $35.00

1509 Queen Ann Dinner Plate, top view. 10-1/2" d, 5-7/8" dcc. $120.00

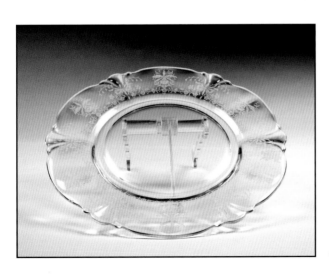

1509 Queen Ann Dinner Plate, side view showing the depth of the pattern.

1519 Waverly Dinner Plate, top view. 10-1/2" d, 6-1/8" dcc. $129.00

1519 Waverly Dinner Plate, side view showing the depth of the pattern.

1519 Waverly Demi Torte Plate.
0-13/16" h, 10-3/4 d. $150.00

1509 Queen Ann, 11 inch Sandwich Plate.
0-3/4" h, 10-7/8" d, 6-1/2" dcc. $150.00

1509 Queen Ann, 12 inch, two-handled Sandwich Plate.
12 d, 6 dcc, two 1-3/8" handles. $170.00

1509 Queen Ann Sandwich Plate. 12 d, centered 'T' handle. $170.00

1519 Waverly 12 inch Salver or Cake Plate, pedestal foot. 3-1/4"
h, 13 d, 5-3/8" db, 2 h pedestal. $240.00

1519 Waverly 13-1/2" inch Salver or Cake Plate, pedestal foot.
2-3/4" h, 14 d, 5-1/4" db, 1-3/4 h pedestal. $240.00

1519 Waverly 14 inch Sandwich Plate. 13 d, 4 dcc. $125.00

1519 Waverly Sandwich Plate with Crestina handle. 14 d, with centered, 4" h, handle. $125.00

1519 Waverly Sandwich Plate with Crestina handle. 14-1/4" d, with centered, 4-1/2" h, handle. $125.00

485 14 inch Sandwich Plate. *Not illustrated.* $125.00

485 14 inch Torte Plate. 14 d. $125.00

1519 Waverly 14 inch Torte Plate.
0-7/8" h, 14 d, 4 dcc. $125.00

1519 Waverly Torte Plate, rolled edge.
1" h, 14 d, 4 dcc, rolled edge. $125.00

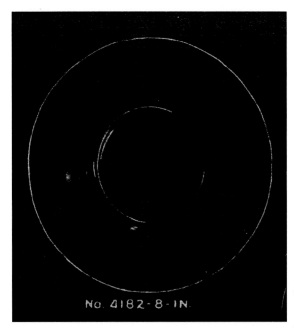

No. 4182-8-IN.

4182 Thin Plate. This came in 6" d, 7" d, and 8" d in Orchid Etch. Image from company brochure.

1509 Queen Ann Cheese Dish. 2-7/8" h, 5-3/8" each side. $60.00

1509 Queen Ann 11 inch Sandwich Plate, 11 d, 6-1/4" dcc. $100.00

Assembled 1509 Queen Ann Cheese Dish and Sandwich Plate, $160.00

1509 Queen Ann 12 inch Cheese & Cracker Plate. 12 d. Note the 3-5/8" d raised ring. $60.00

1509 Queen Ann Cheese Dish & Cracker Plate, assembled. $160.00

1519 Waverly 14 inch Cheese & Cracker Plate. 14 d, 4 dcc. $100.00

1519 Waverly 14 inch Cheese & Cracker Plate, assembled. $160.00

1509 Queen Ann 15 inch Snack Rack Plate, new. 15 d, 3 dcc. $180.00

1509 Queen Ann 16 inch, Snack
Rack Plate. 16 d, 3 dcc. $180.00

Bowls

Epergne with a 5 h vase.

3309 Finger Bowl. 2-1/4" h, 4-3/8" dt, 2-3/8" db. $210.00

1495 Fern Twin Mayonnaise Bowl. 2-3/4" h, 6-1/2" L 5-1/4" dt, one handle, 2 compartments. $70.00

1495 Fern Twin Mayonnaise Bowl and Underplate, assembled. $150.00

1495 Fern Whipped Cream Bowl. 2-1/2" h, 5-1/4" w x 6-1/2" l, with one handle. $80.00

1495 Fern Whipped Cream Bowl and Underplate, assembled. $160.00

1509 Queen Ann 7 inch Triplex Round Relish. 7 d, with 3 compartments and 3 handles. $60.00

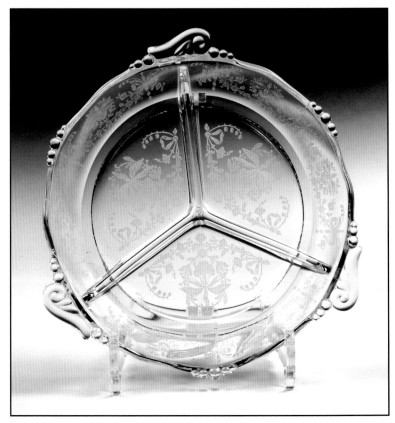

1519 Waverly 7 inch Triplex Round Relish Dish. 7-1/2" d, with 3 compartments and 3 handles. $60.00

1519 Waverly 9 inch Round Relish Dish. 9 d, with 4 compartments and 2 handles. $90.00

1519 Waverly 8 inch Round Relish Dish. 8 d, with 4 compartments and 2 handles. $90.00

1519 Waverly Oval Relish Dish, 1-5/8" h, 7-7/8" w x 11-5/8" l, with 3 compartments. $55.00

1509 Queen Ann 12 inch oblong Celery Dish. 2" h, 4-1/2" w x 11-7/16" l. $60.00

1495 Fern 11-inch Rectangle Relish Dish with 3 compartments and 2 handles. 7-1/2" w x 11" l. *Not illustrated.*

1509 Queen Ann 11-inch 5 O'clock Relish. 7-1/2" w x 11" l. *Not illustrated*

1519 Waverly 11-inch Oval Relish, three compartments. *Not illustrated.*

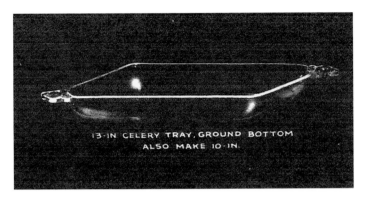

1519 Waverly 13 inch Celery Tray Rectangle, single compartment and 2 handles on diagonally opposite corners. This image is from a company catalog, showing the shape without the Orchid Etch.

1519 Waverly 11 inch Oval Bowl, 4 footed. 3" h, 6" w x 11" l; with little peg-like feet. $150.00

1509 Queen Ann 7 inch Lily Bowl. 3-1/4" h, 6-7/8" d. $90.00

1509 Queen Ann Oval Dressing Bowl with 2 compartments and 2 handles. Straight divider near height of bowl. 2-1/4" h, 5" w x 6-1/2" l. $70.00

1519 Waverly Dressing Bowl with curved divider and 2 handles. The divider is about half the height of the bowl. 2-1/2" h, 5" w x 6-1/2" l. $70.00

485 Salad Bowl, 9 inch. No picture. Shown is a Waverly 9 inch bowl that lacks the smooth rim characteristic of the 485 pieces. $100.00

1509 Queen Ann 9 d, Sunburst Bowl. 2-1/2" h, 9-1/4" d, 3-3/4" db. $60.00

1509 QueenAnn 10 d Sunburst Floral Bowl. 3" h, 9-3/4 d. $60.00

1519 Waverly Floral Bowl, crimped. 4-7/8" h, 9-3/4 d. $70.00

1519 Waverly Floral Bowl, crimped. 3-1/2" h, 10-1/2" d. $75.00

1509 Queen Ann Floral Bowl, crimped. 3-1/2" h, 10-1/2" d. $75..00

1519 Waverly Toast and Dome. *Not illustrated.*

1509 Queen Ann 4-1/2" inch Nappy, 1-5/8" h, 4-1/2" d. $100.00.

1509 Queen Ann 5-1/2" inch Mint Bowl. 1-3/4" h, 5-1/2" d, 2 handles, 4 dolphin feet. $40.00

1509 Queen Ann Jelly Bowl. 1-3/4" h, 6 d, 2 handles 4 dolphin feet. $45.00

1509 Queen Ann Mint Bowl. 2-1/4" h, 5-1/2" d, 3 dolphin feet. $45.00

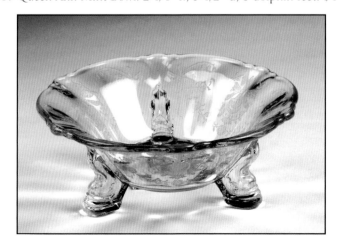

1509 Queen Ann Mint Bowl. 2" h, 5-5/8" d, 3 dolphin feet. $45.00

1509 Queen Ann Souvenir Bowl, Lion's Club 1920-1950. 2-1/4" h, 5-5/8" d, 3 dolphin feet. $55.00

1509 Queen Ann 7-1/2" inch Sauce Bowl. 3" h, 7-1/2" d, 3 dolphin feet. $60.00.

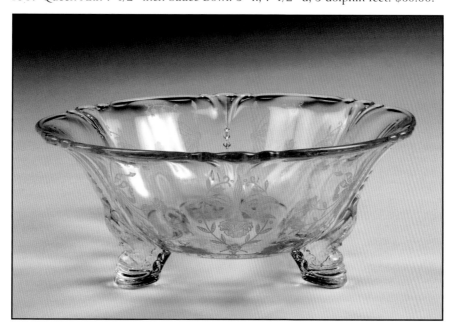

1509 Queen Ann 8 inch Mint Bowl. 2-3/4" h, 7-11/16" d, 3 dolphin feet. $60.00

1509 Queen Ann 8-1/4" inch Floral Bowl with flared top. 8-1/4" d. $50.00

1509 Queen Ann Floral Bowl. 3" h, 8-1/4" d, 2 handles, four dolphin feet. $50.00

1519 Waverly Floral Bowl. 3-1/2" h, 10-1/2" d, 3 seahorse feet. $120.00

1519 Waverly Floral Bowl. 4" h, 11 d, 3 seahorse feet. $120.00

1519 Waverly Floral Bowl, ground bottom. 3-1/2" h, 12-1/2" d. $125.00

1519 Waverly Floral Bowl, crimped. 3" h, 12 d. $100.00

1519 Waverly Floral Bowl. 3" h, 12-1/2" d. $100.00

1519 Waverly Salad Bowl, flared with pedestal foot. 5-1/2" h, 11 d. $80.00

1519 Waverly Bowl, flared with pedestal foot. 5-1/4" h, 11 d. $100.00

1519 Waverly Floral Bowl with pedestal. 4-3/4" h, 11-1/2" d. $100.00

1519 Waverly Mayonnaise Bowl, 1 handle. *Not illustrated.*

1519 Waverly Whipped Cream Bowl, 1 handle. *Not illustrated.*

1519 Waverly 5-1/2" inch Mayonnaise & Spoon, with
pedestal foot. 3-1/4" h, 5-1/2" dt, 2-1/4" db. $65.00

1519 Waverly Mayonnaise, Spoon, & Plate. Note that
the Mayonnaise Plate has a raised rim. $65.00

1519 Waverly 6-1/2" inch Jelly Bowl with pedestal foot. 2-3/4" h, 6-1/2" d. $65.00

1509 Queen Ann 6-3/4 inch Jelly Bowl with fan foot. 2-1/4" h, 6-3/4 d. $60.00

1509 Queen Ann Berry Bowl. 3" h, 6" dt, 4 dcc. $150.00

1509 Queen Ann 9 inch Gardenia Bowl. 1-3/4" h, 9-1/2" d, 3-3/4 dcc. $100.00.

1519 Waverly 10 inch, Gardenia Bowl. 2" h, 9-1/2" d, 4 dcc. $100.00

485 12 inch Gardenia Bowl. 2-1/4" h, 12 d, 4-1/4" dcc Note smooth rim. $125.00

1519 Waverly 13 inch Gardenia Bowl. 1-5/8" h, 13 d, 4 dcc. $125.00

1519 Waverly 13 inch Gardenia Bowl and integrated candleholder.
2" h, 13 d, with included candleholder.

1519 Waverly Gardenia Bowl & 6 inch, Epergne. 13" d, 2-1/2" h, (3-3/4 h with Epergne). A 6-1/2" inch Epergne was also made, but is not pictured. The center of the Epergne can hold a candle or a 5, 6, or 7 inch 4233 vase.

1519 Waverly Gardenia Bowl & 5 inch 4233 Vase. 13 d, overall height 6-1/2" inches. The Waverly Gardenia Bowl with the 4233 vase was not included in the numbering system, but they make a nice combination and are shown here in two sizes.

1519 Waverly Gardenia Bowl & 6 inch 4233 Vase.

1519 Waverly 13 inch Gardenia Bowl & 5-1/2" inch Epergne and Vase.

1187 Yeoman 9-1/2" inch Epergne with candleholder. 3-1/2" h, 9-1/2" d, 5" db, pedestal foot. $320.00

1187 Yeoman with Vase. 9-1/2" d, 5" db, 8" h, vase 5 h.

1187 Yeoman with Vase. 9-1/2" d, 5" db, 10" h, vase 7 h.

1519 Waverly Fruit Centerpiece Candleholder. This could hold an epergne or vase. *Not Illustrated.*

Miscellaneous Forms

1509 Queen Ann Mustard Jar and Lid. 2.35 h overall, 1-3/8" h at lid line, 1-1/2" d. $21.00

4121 Marmalade Jar and Lid. 4-1/2" h overall, 3-1/2" h at lid line 3-1/8" d. $225.00

1519 Waverly Oil
Bottle, 3 oz. 8-3/8" h,
2-1/2" mxd. $200.00

5031 French Dressing
Bottle 8 oz. 6" h, 2-1/
8" mxd. $110.00

1489 Puritan 4 inch Cigarette Box (1-9/16" h, 2-13/16" w x 4" l) *Not Illustrated.*

1519 Waverly Butter Dish with horse head finial. Base: 6-1/2" d, 3-1/2" square center. Dome: 5" h, 3-1/2" square lid. $125.00

1951 Cabachon Butterdish for a quarter pound stick. Base: 1" h, 3" w x 7" l. Cover: 2-1/2" w x 5-3/8" l, 2-1/4" h. Overall height: 2-3/8". $395.00

No. 5022—6 in.
Low Foot Candy Box
& Cover W/O

5022 Graceful 6 inch Candy Dish with Lid, low footed. Image from company catalog.

1519 Chocolate Bowl and
Cover with Seashell handle
and Crestina fnial. 2-1/2" h,
5" dt, 2-5/8" db. $80.00

1519 Waverly Chocolate Bowl with Bow Knot handle. 5-1/2" h, 2-1/2" h
at lid line, 6.19" dt, 2-1/2" db $110.00.

1519 Waverly Candy Jar with Seahorse handles. 8-1/2" h,
5-1/4" h, at lid line 5" dt, 4" db, pedestal feet. $125.00.

1519 Waverly 6 inch Lemon Bowl & Cover with Dolphin finial. 4" h, 1-1/2" h at lid line, 4-1/2" w x 5" l. $115.00. Also made in a 6 inch size, not shown.

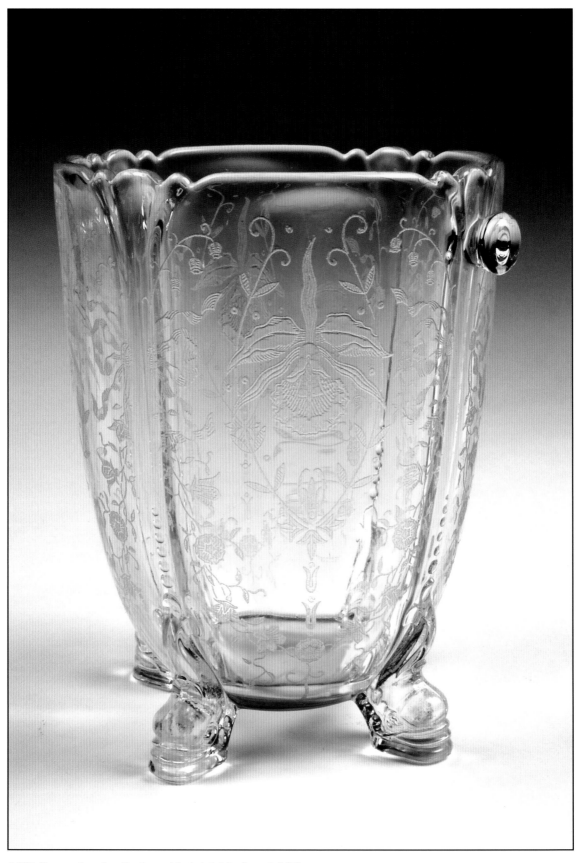

1509 Queen Ann Ice Bucket with 4 dolphin feet. 6-1/2"
h, 5-1/4" d, (missing handle and tongs). $ 425.00

1519 Waverly Ice Bucket with Crestina handles. 4-1/4" h, 6-1/2" dt, 3-1/2" db. $425.00

4035 Cigarette Holder. 3-7/16" h, 2" dt, 1-3/4 square base. $55.00

1519 Waverly Cigarette Holder and Lid with Seahorse handles.
5-3/4" h, 3" h, at Lid 2-3/8" d. $125.00

3303 Shrimp Cocktail Icers and Liners.
2.94" h, 3-1/2" dt, 4" db. $225.00

1519 Waverly Comport with pedestal foot.
3-3/4" h, 6 d. $65.00

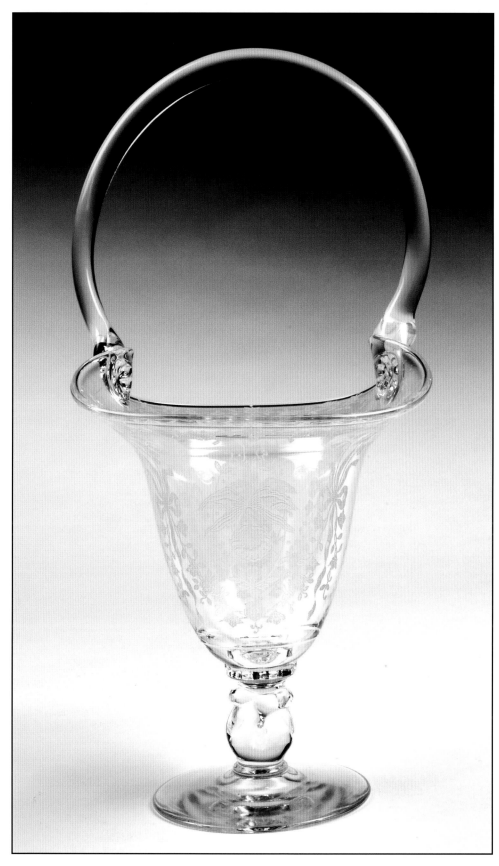

1540 Lariat Basket. 10 h overall , 6" h, at handle
4" w x 6" l, 3" db. $305.00

1519 Waverly Sugar and Creamer. Sugar: 4-1/8" h, 3-1/2" w x 4" l. Cream:
4-1/8" h, 3-1/4" w x 4-3/8" l. Both have octagon bases. $65.00

1509 Queen Ann Tray for Individual Sugar and Creamer.
4-1/4" x 8". $50.00

1519 Waverly Sugar and Creamer. 2.94" h, 2-1/2" w x 3" l. Round base. $65.00

1519 Waverly Sugar, Cream and Queen Ann Tray. $110.00

42 Salt and Pepper. 4-1/8" h, 1-1/4" mxd, 1-1/2" db, with pedestal foot. $115.00

57 Salt and Pepper (not etched). 4-1/4" h, 2-1/2" d of hexagonal base, 1" dt. These pieces
were produced with the Orchid Etch, but were not available for photography.

1519 Waverly Salt and Pepper (not etched). 3-1/8" h, 2 w, (1-5/8" deep, front to back). When found in Orchid Etch, $60.00. This piece was produced with the Orchid Etch, but was not available for photography.

1519 Waverly Salt and Pepper with pedestal feet. 4" h, 1-7/8" mxd, 1-3/4" db. $65.00

Comparison Salt and Peppers, models 42, 57, Waverly, 3" h, and Waverly, 4 h

1519 Waverly Oval Comport with pedestal foot. 5-1/4"
h, 4-1/2" db, 4-3/8" w by 7-1/4" l. $125.00

1519 Waverly Oval Nut Comport with pedestal foot. 4-1/4" h, 2-1/4" db, 4-3/8" w by 6-1/2" L. $125.00

Comparison of Oval Comport and Oval Nut Comport.

1951 Cabachon Candy Dish. 4-1/8" h, 6 d, 2 h at lid line. $150.00

1540 Lariat 5 inch Mayonnaise with rolled edge and pedestal foot. *Not Illustrated.*

Cocktails & Pitchers

3484 Donna Half Gallon Jug. 9-1/2" h, 3-3/4 d at 7" h,
5 d at 2-1/4" h, 4-1/4" db. $175.00

4036 Quart Cocktail Shaker in original factory wrap. 12-1/2" h, 2-1/2" d at 8-3/4" h, 3-1/4" db. $225.00

4036.5 Pint Decanter. 8-1/2" h at stopper, 2-1/16" dt, 1-1/8" d at 8" h, 3-3/8" d at 2-1/2" h, 2-1/4" db. $225.00

4037 (4036) Pint Oval Sherry. 8" h, 6 h at stopper,
2 d, 2-7/8" w x 6-1/4" l. $225.00

4164 Ice Jug, 73 oz. 8" h, 4-3/4" dt, 6 d at 3" h, 4-1/2" db $225.00

4225 Cobel Cocktail Shaker, 1-pint, with Ram stopper. 12" h, 2-3/4 d, 3-3/4" db. $250.00

4225 Cobel Cocktail Shaker. 1-quart, with Rooster stopper. 15" h, 3-1/2" d, 4" db. $225.00

Comparison of Cobel Quart & Pint Cocktail Shakers.

5032 Half-gallon Ice Tankard. 11-1/2" h, 4-3/8" dt, 4" db. $900.00

Vases

1519 Waverly 4 inch Violet
Vase. 3-3/4" h, 4 d.
$155.00

4045 Ball Vase in Alexandrite.
6-1/2" h, 7 d. This pattern
came in Orchid Etch but was
unavailable for photography.
$125.00 in Orchid Etch.

1519 Waverly Round Vase. 6-3/4" h, 3-3/4" dt, 3" db. $95.00

1519 Waverly Fan Vase. 7" h, 3-1/16" db, 1-3/8" w x 6" L. $125.00

1540 Lariat Vase No. 1, straight. 7-5/16" h, 4-1/2" h,
1.6275 d at 2" h, 4-1/4" db. $65.00

1540 Lariat Vase No. 2, fan. 7-7/8" h, 4-1/8" db, 1-3/4 w by 6 L. $75.00

1540 Lariat Vase No. 3, square crimped top. 7.19" h, 4 sq top 1-3/4 d at 2-1/4" h, 4-1/4" db. $75.00

1540 Lariat Vase No. 4, crimped top. 7-1/4" h, 4-1/2" dt,
1-3/4 d at 2-1/4" h, 4-1/4" db. $75.00

1540 Lariat Vase No.5, crimped top. 5-13/16" h, 2-3/8" d at 2-1/4" h, 2-15/16" db. $75.00

1540 Lariat Vase No. 6, crimped fan. 6-7/8" h, 5-1/8" db, 1-3/4 w by 5-3/4 L. $75.00

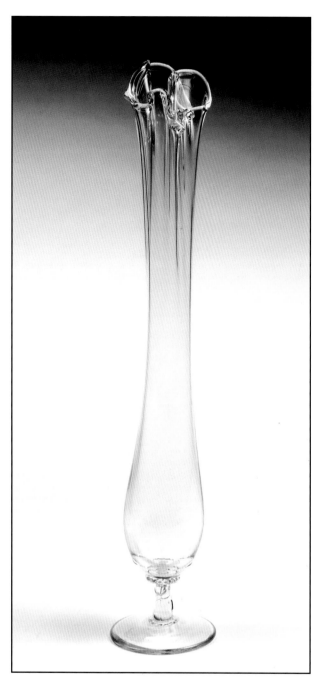

1540 Lariat Vase No. 7. Under 12 h. Also came as Lariat Vase No. 8 at 15-1/2" h., 2-1/2" d midway, 3" dt. This vase came in Orchid Etch at both sizes, but was unavailable for photography. $115.00 if etched.

4057 Flip Vase. 10-3/4" h, 6" dt, 3-3/4" db. $275.00

4191 Vase with pedestal foot. Came in 6 inch, 8 inch, and 12 inch sizes. The image showing the shape is from a company catalog, but does not show the Orchid Etching.

4192.5+ Vase, 9 inch. 9-1/2" h, 4-1/4" dt, 4" db.

4198 Vase, 8 inch. 8-1/4" h, 3-1/2" dt, 3-1/2" db, 2-1/2" d at 4 h. $200.00. This vase also came in a 10 inch size, which was unavailable for photography. $200.00.

4198 Vase 12 inch. 12" h, 5" dt, 5" db, 3-1/2" d at 5-1/2" h. $250.00. This vase also came in a 14 inch size, which was unavailable for phtoography.

Comparison of 4198 vases, 8 and 12 inch

4205 Bud Vase, 9 inch. 9-1/2" h, 3-3/16" dt, 1-1/2" dat 6-1/2" h, 2-1/4" d at 5-1/4" h, 0.6275 d at 1" h, 3-15/16" db. $245.00

5012 Urn Bud Vase, 8 inch with square base. 8-3/16" h, 3-3/8" dt, 2 square base. $300.00

5012 Urn Bud Vase, 10 inch, with square base. 10" h, 2-5/8" dt, 2 square base. $300.00. This vase also came in a 12 inch size, which was unavailable for photography. $350.00.

Comparison of 8 and 10 inch 5012 Urn Bud Vases

148

5012 Urn Vase, 9 inch, with square base. 9-1/2" h, 6" dt, 4 Sq base. $900.00

5034 Vase, 7 inch. *Not illustrated.*

Candleholders

112 Mercury Candleholder, one light. 3-3/8" h, 1-1/2" dt, 4.81" db. $45.00

134 Trident Candleholder, two lights. 5-1/2" h, 5-1/2" db. $60.00

1519 Waverly Candleholder, two lights. 5-1/2" h, 5-1/2" db. $100.00

142 Cascade Candleholder, three lights. 5-3/4" h, 5-1/4" db. $100.00

1495 Fern Candleholder, two lights. 5-3/4" h, 5-1/4" db. $100.00

1519 Waverly Candleholder, three lights. 7" h, 5-1/2" db, 8-5/8". $100.00

1509 Queen Ann Candelabra, one light. 8-1/4" h, 3-7/8" db, 5" db, eight prism. $100.00

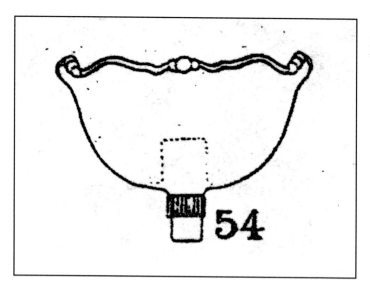

1519 Waverly Epergnette. 6-1/2" d.
Image from company catalog, shown
without Orchid Etching.

1519 Waverly Epergnette. 5-1/2" h,
2-1/2" h, 3-1/4" h, including the
stem. $20.00.

1519 Waverly Epergnette. 6"
h, 2-1/2" h, 3-1/4" h, including the stem. $20.00

1615 Flame Candleholder. 10-3/4" h, 5-1/2" db; 6" h, at candleholders. $75.00

1519 Waverly, one light plume. 4-1/2" h. Image from company catalog, shown without Orchid Etching.

026 Blown glass candleholder, one light. *Not illustrated.*

1503 Crystaline Hurricane Light with square base. *Not illustrated.*

Index